ZEN

~ as ~

F*CK

Shine on, MOTHERFUCKER

Today is YOUR fucking day!

MAY YOUR CUP RUNNETH *the* FUCK OVER

SPREAD THOSE BEAUTIFUL *Fucking Wings*

LET THAT SHIT GO

IT'S A
BRILLIANT
FUCKING DAY!

CARPE Fucking DiEM

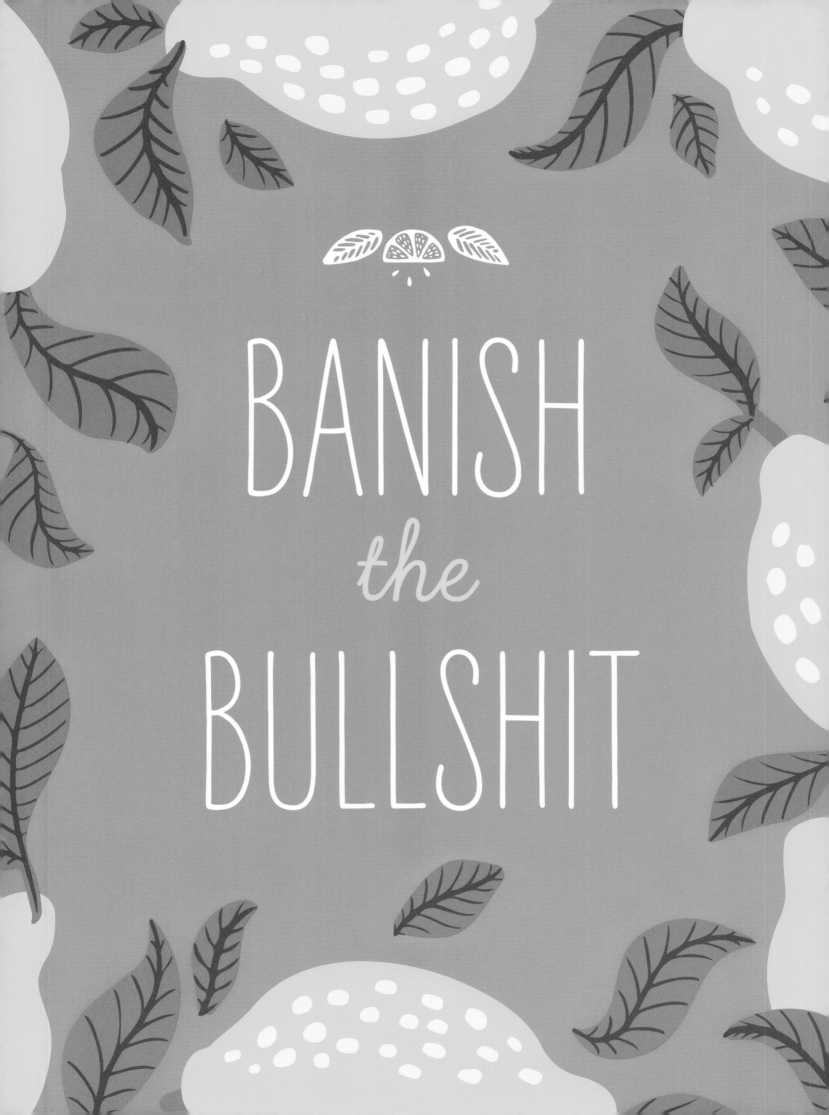

BANISH

the

BULLSHIT

YOU CAN FUCKING DO IT!

You are my FUCKING SUNSHINE!